Last Night I Danced with a Stranger

with a Stranger

A Guide to Dream Analysis

by KIRSTEN HALL

BLACK DOG
& LEVENTHAL
PUBLISHERS
NEW YORK

TABLE OF CONTENTS

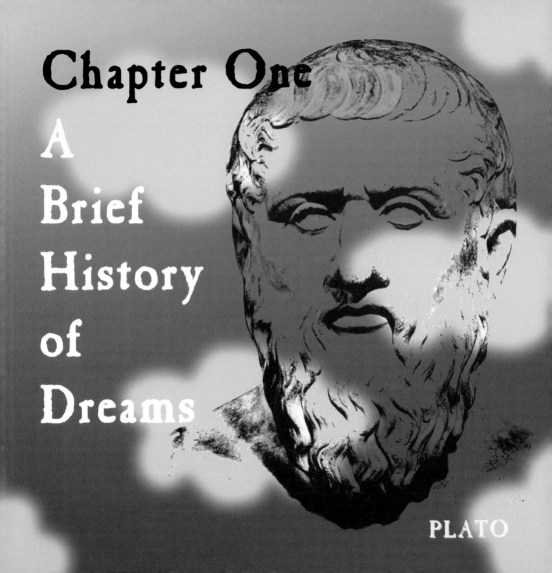

Chapter One

A Brief History of Dreams

PLATO

A BRIEF
HISTORY
OF
DREAMS

A BRIEF HISTORY OF DREAMS

Tales from long ago reveal the same curiosity about dreams that exists in today's world. Although theories about dreams have varied around the world and throughout time, people's fascination with dreams has not.

ANCIENT CIVILIZATIONS

Ancient Egyptians valued dreams for their prophetic messages, and dream incubation was a common practice. During dream incubation, people spent nights in special sleep temples where priests were on hand to interpret dreams.

Dreams played a significant role in ancient Greek culture as well. People of all classes, from kings to simple merchants, visited the oracle at Delphi for interpretations of their dreams. Like the ancient Egyptians, the Greeks considered dreams to be messages from the gods. The Greeks also constructed temples for sleep. People spent as long as several weeks there, working with priests in an effort to understand the messages from their gods.

Famous Greek philosophers from Homer (in the eighth century B.C.) through Plato (in the fourth century B.C.), continued to believe and teach that dreams were vehicles for divine manifestation. However, a debate emerged when another philosopher, a student at Plato's Academy named Aristotle, introduced the revolutionary concept that dreams were not messages from gods at all. Instead, he argued that dreams were the mind's effort to process certain events happening in the dreamer's life. He also believed that dreams reflected the state of the dreamer's physical health.

In the third century B.C., Hippocrates, often considered to be the founder of modern medicine, also believed that dreams could facilitate the diagnosis of human illness. Arguing that sound body was reflected by sound mind, Hippocrates felt that troublesome dreams could be related to physical illness.

Homer

This theory persisted among Greek physicians through the second century A.D.

Ancient Romans also had theories about dreams. In A.D. 150, a Roman physician named Artemidorus wrote the first extensive collection of books on dream analysis. It was entitled Oneirocritica, which means "The Interpretation of Dreams." About 200 years later, the second Oneirocritica was published by Astrampsychus, further elaborating on the theme.

BIBLICAL DREAMS

The Bible is rich with references to dreams in which God reveals himself to certain chosen people. Among the most famous examples are Jacob's dream of a ladder on which angels traveled back and forth between heaven and earth and Joseph's dream predicting the famine in Egypt. In the Book of Lamentations, God becomes angry and decides to punish people by withholding their ability to dream.

> *J*acob dreamed and behold a ladder set up on the earth, and the top of it reached to heaven: and behold the angels of God ascending and descending on it.
>
> Genesis 28:12

13

MODERN TIMES

In the eighteenth and nineteenth centuries, dreams continued to influence many famous and accomplished people.

Numerous writers have credited their dreams as the inspiration for some of their important works. Samuel Taylor Coleridge's famous poem *Kubla Khan* came to him in a dream; after he awakened, he started writing down the hundreds of lines that had already been formed in his dream. Unfortunately, Coleridge had only written down 54 lines when someone knocked on his door, interrupting him and causing him to forget the rest of the poem. More recently, musician Paul McCartney claims to have dreamt the tune to his famous hit "Yesterday."

Dreams have also had a major impact on the field of modern science. Albert Einstein claims to have dreamt up the theory of relativity. Niels Bohr, world-renowned physicist, refined his theory on the

Samuel Taylor Coleridge

movement of electrons in a dream. Dreams have affected the art world as well. Followers of an artistic movement called Romanticism believed that artists had the power to destroy the barrier between dreams and reality through their work. Surrealists such as André Breton felt that the unconscious mind, where he believed dreams came from, was responsible for the creation of all artwork. Artistic geniuses Salvador Dali and Pablo Picasso both credited dreams as the inspiration for some of their greatest masterpieces.

So, what do dreams mean to people today? There is an entire branch of science devoted to answering this question. Dream analysis has become increasingly popular and is practiced more commonly then ever before. Major corporations now conduct seminars on studying dreams. Dream institutes offering dream-analysis workshops are on the rise. Stores sell aromatherapy products that promise to bring "sweet dreams."

What do your dreams mean? How can they serve you? Don't try to answer just yet! First, let's take a

Dreams are faithful interpreters of our inclinations; but there is art required to sort and understand them.

Montaigne, "Of Experience" in *Essays*

quick look at the two most important dream theorists in modern history. We'll return to the questions later.

SIGMUND FREUD

Sigmund Freud, the father of psychoanalysis, revolutionized how we perceive dreams. Born in 1856, Freud grew up in Austria during the Victorian era, a time when discussing sex was considered taboo. Freud, however, spent much time theorizing about the sexual desires of people and how those desires manifested themselves in a sexually repressive society. After studying neurology for several years at the University of Vienna, Freud began to refine his theories about the struggle between our sexual desires and the guilt that we feel as a result of those desires.

Freud claimed that dreams were a means by which the unconscious struggle between guilt and desire attempted to resolve itself. Dreaming was an opportunity for a person to seek "wish fulfillment" in ways that were impossible during the waking hours.

Sigmund Freud

17

Queen Katherine's Dream, William Blake

Dreams are a drama taking place on one's own interior stage.

Carl Jung

In dreams, our attempts at fulfilling these desires were safe. They were personal and private and were, in fact, not even real. Freud went on to theorize that our deepest and most repressed desires were concealed by bizarre and often confusing symbols in our dreams. By close examination of the peculiar imagery in dreams, one could attempt to understand their meanings.

Objects in dreams were often phallic to Freud. If one were to dream of a candlestick, for instance, Freud might claim that the dreamer was really concealing his or her preoccupation with male genitalia. Likewise, if one of his patients dreamt of a coffee mug, Freud might contend that he or she had actually been envisioning a woman's vagina.

Freud's insistence on interpreting the imagery in most dreams in a strictly sexual way—leaving no room for any other possible explanation—cost him the support of many, including his closest colleague, fellow psychoanalyst Carl Jung.

CARL JUNG

Carl Jung, a Swiss scientist, was nearly 20 years younger than Freud. When the two met, they became fast friends. Freud served as Jung's mentor and greatly enjoyed the young man's curiosity, intelligence and inquisitive nature. Ironically, it was the qualities Freud so enjoyed in his colleague that later led to the demise of their friendship.

Jung concurred with the foundation of Freud's dream-analysis theory. That is, he agreed that dreams are manifestations of the unconscious mind—the part of the psyche that holds the feelings and drives of which one is normally unaware. (The term "subconscious" refers to partial consciousness, drives and feelings that one is somewhat aware of.) Eventually, however, differences arose between Freud's and Jung's theories.

Carl Jung

<blockquote>
I've always had access to other worlds. We all do because we all dream.

Leonora Carrington, twentieth century surrealist painter
</blockquote>

<blockquote>20</blockquote>

SEXUAL DESIRE VS. A COLLECTIVE UNCONSCIOUS

Freud, as mentioned before, contended that dreams almost always portrayed sexual longings (often dating back to infancy) that the dreamer was suppressing, and that these sexual longings were concealed in dreams through bizarre imagery. Freud, therefore, thought dreams were a way of further suppressing one's true feelings. It was Freud's opinion that many dreams were an expression of psychic illness, usually stemming from these repressed desires.

Jung, on the other hand, believed dreams were not necessarily sexual in nature. Furthermore, he believed the imagery in dreams was not meant to suppress thoughts and feelings, but rather to expose them. Jung thought dreams were messages from the unconscious to the conscious mind. It was Jung's opinion that, far from expressing psychic illness, dreams were often sources of guidance, comfort and inspiration. He contended that dreams could shed light on one's aspirations and help facilitate their fulfillment.

The Dream of Innocent III. Giotto

Besides believing in everyone having his or her own personal unconscious, Jung contended there was a "collective unconscious" that consisted of common images and memories shared by all humans. The collective unconscious can be seen as the natural instincts one is born with—for example, a baby's inborn knowledge that it must seek care and nourishment from its mother. Jung used the term "archetype" to describe the common images that everyone is born with a knowledge of. He believed these images manifested themselves in people's dreams. Archetypal images include the mother, the father, the child and the hero. See the dream dictionary in Chapter Six for more information on what these images mean.

Finally, while Freud believed dreams were reflective of one's past, Jung believed they could actually give us clues as to what will take place in the future.

Who do you agree with—Freud or Jung? Why or why not? Most likely, you were able to see validity in both their theories. For, you see, the world is not black or white. Likewise, it sometimes is difficult for us to clearly delineate between our waking and sleeping lives since they are so elusively but unmistakably linked. Perhaps the scientist/philosopher/mathematician René Descartes said it best when he wondered aloud whether waking life was also really just a dream.

*D*eeds
cannnot
dream what
dreams can
do.

e. e. cummings

Chapter Two

Sleep Stages and Cycles

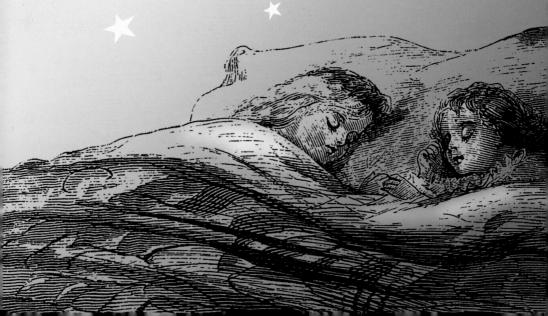

CHAPTER TWO:

SLEEP STAGES AND CYCLES

I love to sleep. I sleep through thunderstorms and phone calls, and often, even my alarm clock. In a family of workaholics who view sleep as a mere necessity and think four to six hours of shut-eye a night should suffice, I am a true oddball. Do I mind the teasing I endure as a result of my ongoing love affair with the pillow? No way! Not when Albert Einstein himself slept for 12 hours nightly. How does that saying go—great minds sleep alike?

Each one of us has his or her own sleep cycle. Some people are up with the sun and rest when it sets. Other people are night owls who find working the graveyard shift ideal. Some people need to sleep for just six hours to wake feeling refreshed. Still others need at least ten hours of sleep before they are able to haul themselves out of bed. (Most people sleep an average of eight hours a night.) It is best if you have a schedule that permits you to live in tune with your natural sleep-wake cycle. If not, it is possible to change your body clock to match your schedule: If you force yourself to wake up and go to bed on a new schedule, your body will eventually get used to it and adopt the new schedule. Interestingly, scientists

Il Sogno Dell'Innamorato, Hieronymus Bosch

> *I* dream, therefore I exist.
>
> J. August Strindberg,
> Swedish dramatist,
> novelist and poet

have found that people with outgoing personalities have an easier time changing their sleep-wake cycle than do shy people. Also, younger people have an easier time adjusting their body clock to fit their schedule than do older people.

THE STAGES OF SLEEP

While we are asleep we go through a cycle of five sleep stages. Stage One is a light sleep in which the sleeper may have hallucinatory experiences, such as a sensation of falling. After about five minutes, Stage Two takes over. Stage Two is a deeper form of sleep than Stage One. However, a person can be easily awakened during Stage Two.

After about 20 minutes, the sleeper goes through a brief transition (Stage Three) into a very deep sleep (Stage Four). It is hard to wake a person up when he or she is in Stage Four sleep. Ironically, Stage Four is when sleepwalking, sleeptalking and night terrors (see Chapter Three) can occur. Also, during Stage Four a growth hormone is released into the body and bodily tissues are repaired. Stage Four lasts for

Illustration from *Alice's Adventures in Wonderland*, Arthur Rackham

*I*n bed my real love has always been the sleep that rescued me by allowing me to dream.

Silia in *The Rules of the Game*, Luigi Pirandello, Italian author and playwright

about half an hour; then the sleeper goes back through Stages Three and Two, but instead of waking up, enters the fascinating sleep phase of REM.

REM sleep is when dreams occur. REM stands for "rapid eye movement"—when people dream, their eyes remain closed but dart about rapidly. A person in REM sleep has brain waves similar to the waking state. Breathing becomes rapid and blood pressure rises. However, the muscles become very relaxed—so relaxed, in fact, that when people dream, they are basically paralyzed. Some scientists speculate this is so the sleeper will not act out the events in the dream. The first episode of REM sleep (the first dream) lasts about ten minutes. Then the sleeper drifts back down to Stage Two sleep and begins the sleep cycle again. The sleep cycle repeats itself every 90 minutes, with the non-REM stages becoming shorter and the REM stages becoming longer. The dreams one has during the night may have the same theme or be different from one another. Almost 25 percent of each night's sleep is spent dreaming. Therefore, the average person spends a total of about four years of his or her life dreaming!

It is still unclear why people (and other mammals) dream, but it is clear we need to dream—when deprived of REM sleep during one night, people have increased REM sleep the next night. A good night's sleep is necessary to feel good and function at one's best during the day.

TIPS FOR A GOOD NIGHT'S SLEEP—AND GOOD DREAMS

Do you ever have times when—by the clock—you got enough sleep, but you still don't feel rested? There are several possible reasons for your grogginess. We will examine some of these reasons in the following list of sleeping tips. Then take the review quiz to find out how much you've learned.

1. Don't have a nightcap before going to bed. Many doctors advise that you refrain from drinking alcohol for at least three hours before you hit the sack. Why? Because alcohol disturbs your natural sleep cycle and decreases the amount of time you spend in REM sleep, when dreams occur.

Hope is a waking dream.

Aristotle,
Diogenes Laertius,
Lives of Eminent Philosophers

31

2. Don't have coffee (unless it's decaffeinated) immediately before bedtime. Also avoid tea, soda, and chocolate, since they contain caffeine as well. Caffeine, like alcohol, interferes with REM sleep. Caffeine also makes it difficult for most people to fall asleep to begin with—so have that espresso at least five or six hours before you go to bed.

3. Maybe that waitress screwed up your order for decaf and gave you regular coffee. Or maybe you suffer from periodic insomnia. For whatever reason, you can't fall asleep. Should you stay in bed and stare at the ceiling, counting sheep? No way. After 15 minutes, go do something. Read a book. Listen to your favorite CD. Feed the cats. You'll soon catch the yawns.

4. Have sex. Sexual activity causes your body to release certain endorphins that help you relax. The more relaxed you are, the easier it will be for you to drift off into la-la land.

> *An immense joy comes when the house of fear collapses and we realize the possibilities of our dreams.*
>
> Alberto Tazco, South American shaman

33

The Starry Night, Vincent Van Gogh

5. Is there any truth to the old wives' tale that a warm glass of milk will help you fall asleep? Yes! Milk contains an amino acid called tryptophan, and tryptophan causes drowsiness. Can you think of a food that makes you sleepy? I'll give you a clue: It's Thanksgiving and there really is a good reason that everyone's too tired to do all those dishes. You guessed it! The tryptophan in turkey makes it a great bedtime snack.

6. Don't smoke. If you haven't already given up this nasty habit, here's yet another reason why you should: cigarettes have an amphetamine-like quality—they increase your heart rate and blood pressure. Once you get all revved up, how do you expect to ever fall asleep? Flush 'em, I tell ya! Use some of the money you save to buy yourself a nice fluffy down pillow. Then you'll sleep tight.

7. Don't engage in strenuous exercise immediately before bedtime. When you exercise, your body fills with adrenaline, making good old rest and relaxation virtually impossible. Many

doctors advise exercising earlier in the day rather than later (not less than two hours before bed time) for this very reason.

8. Ever take a hot shower or bath before going to bed? If not, you should try it. The hot water makes your blood rush to the surface of your skin. Then, when you get into your bed and under the sheets (which are cooler than your skin at this point), your body begins to lose all that heat. The change in temperature makes you feel drowsy. (People with heart problems, however, should consult a physician before making a habit of this.)

9. Speaking of physicians, do you take any prescription (or over-the-counter) drugs? If you are currently taking any medications, they may be disrupting your sleep. If you think your sleeping habits have changed since you began a new medication, be sure to ask your doctor about it.

10. When you are sick or stressed out, you may need more sleep than usual. Allow yourself some

Try to wash your mind before you go to sleep like you brush your teeth; then your dreams will be clear.

Tenzin W. Rinpoche, Tibetan teacher

extra shut-eye at these times. Sleep is part of the healing process.

TO SLEEP OR NOT TO SLEEP—REVIEW QUIZ

1. You're out at dinner with your boss (and she's paying). After a lovely meal and a few carafes of wine, she suggests that you each order an after-dinner drink. She asks for a glass of sambuca. You know that you have to be up early the next morning, but the whole night has been so pleasant and you feel that you two are really bonding. You:
    a. tell the waiter, "Make that two!"
    b. tell the waiter, "Make mine a double!"
    c. tell the waiter, "I'll have herbal tea."

2. You've just come down with a cold and sore throat but are expecting company for dinner. You:
    a. spend the day shopping and cooking.
    b. decide to order take-out.
    c. reschedule the dinner and go to bed early.

Chang's Dream of his beloved visiting from the Western Pavilion, Ch'iu Ying (Ming Dynasty)

*D*reams are a reservoir of knowledge and experience, yet they are often overlooked as a vehicle for exploring reality.

Tibetan teacher Tarthang Tulku, Openness Mind

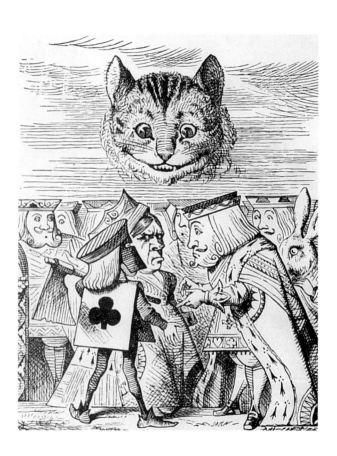

3. It's the middle of the night, and you just can't fall asleep. You:
   a. lie very still.
   b. have a brownie and a cup of hot chocolate.
   c. move to a comfortable chair and snuggle up with a good book.

4. You have to get up early and want to guarantee a good night's sleep. Just before bedtime you:
   a. start to figure out how much you owe for this year's taxes.
   b. drink a cup of hot tea (non-decaf).
   c. have a hot bath.

Option C is the correct answer for all of the questions. If you did not answer C, you'd better work on getting Zzzzz's. If you did answer C throughout, I "C" you've been paying attention. Good job, and I look forward to "C"ing you in the next chapter!

*T*hey who dream by day are cognizant of many things which escape those who dream only by night.

Edgar Allan Poe,
"Eleonora"

The Cheshire Cat and the Queen's Croquet Ground, John Tenniel

Chapter Three

Types of Dreams

CHAPTER THREE:

TYPES OF DREAMS

While it may sometimes be hard to remember a dream you've just had, even moments after waking up, nightmares are often easier to remember than any other kind of dream. People often confuse nightmares with night terrors. Examining the two scenarios below will help us see the difference between a nightmare and a night terror.

Scenario #1:

Franklin puts his five-year-old daughter Mariah to sleep. He goes into the kitchen, heats up the kettle, pours himself a cup of tea, and decides to finish reading the newspaper. About 25 minutes later, Franklin hears Mariah screaming. He rushes down the hall and enters her room to find her kicking her covers and throwing punches in the air. Franklin hurries over to her and gently wakes her up, telling her, "It's just a bad dream, sweetheart. You're just having a bad dream."

Scenario #2:

Franklin puts his five-year-old daughter Mariah to sleep. He's feeling pretty exhausted himself and falls asleep on the couch while reading his newspaper. A few hours later, he wakes up and decides to go to bed. As he passes by Mariah's room, he peeks in and sees she is sound asleep. He gives her a kiss on the forehead and heads to bed himself. The next morning, while eating her pancakes, Mariah tells her father of the bear that escaped from the zoo and chased her all night long in her dreams. Franklin tells her that bears never escape from zoos and she shouldn't worry about that again.

Which of the above is an example of a nightmare and which is an example of a night terror? If you guessed that scenario #1 showed Mariah having a night terror, you are right.

Night terrors are actually quite different from nightmares. In order for a dream to classify as a nightmare, it must take place during REM sleep (for more on REM sleep, see Chapter Two), which does

*D*reams are the touchstones of our characters.

Henry David Thoreau

43

Camelot: How Four Queens Found Sir Lancelot Sleeping, by William Frank Calderon

> # T
> he dream
> is the small
> hidden door in
> the deepest and
> most intimate
> sanctum of the
> soul.
>
> Carl Jung

not occur until at least an hour after falling asleep. Since Mariah had only just drifted off to sleep in scenario #1, we can assume she had not yet entered the REM stage. This would rule out the possibility of her having had a nightmare just yet.

Another distinction between the two is that sleepers do not generally exhibit physical excitement while having a nightmare, though they may during a night terror. Since Mariah was kicking her covers and clenching her fists in scenario #1, we can assume that she was in the midst of a night terror.

A final distinguishing factor between night terrors and nightmares is that dreamers often remember a nightmare they've had in vivid detail. On the other hand, a person who suffers from night terrors will often awaken without any memory of what had seemed so frightening the night before.

WHY DO WE HAVE NIGHTMARES?

We have nightmares when we are anxious or depressed about something. A nightmare can occur because something frightening took place during the day—or a nightmare could express fears hidden in our unconscious.

Take the example of Ann: She usually has pleasant dreams that she enjoys recalling—things such as fun parties and exciting visits to exotic locations. However, one night Ann had a terrible nightmare. She awakes and jumps out of bed. Instead of pausing for a few minutes to savor the experiences in her dream, she does her best to distract herself while she gets ready for work. She doesn't want to remember the nightmare she just had, one in which she was being chased by a creature that was half dog, half human.

What Ann should have realized, however, is that there is a reason she had such a nightmare—her

Why does the eye see a thing more clearly in dreams than the mind while awake?

Leonardo Da Vinci

47

> ## *T*he myth is the public dream and the dream is the private myth.
>
> Joseph Campbell,
> *The Power of Myth*

unconscious was forcing her to recognize feelings she had been denying.

Dreams serve to bring certain emotional issues to our attention when they have been ignored for too long. Just as it is not healthy to ignore a physical illness, we must not ignore the fears and worries our dreams bring to light.

In Ann's case, she had divorced her husband two years earlier. The dog they had raised together stayed with him and Ann felt intensely guilty, as though she had abandoned them. Amy kept herself busy with work and had an active social life. She felt that she had really moved on with her life and had made the right decision by starting over on her own. What Ann didn't realize, however, was that she had not truly dealt with the feelings she had about the divorce.

By examining the nightmare and exploring what may have caused it, Ann might have made important strides in resolving her feelings. But by ignoring the

An Angel Awakens the Prophet Elijah, Juan Antonio Escalante

> **A**ll dreams are given for the benefit of the individual, would he but interpret them correctly.

Edgar Cayce

nightmare, her feelings of guilt will, most likely, continue to surface in her dreams.

As evidenced in this example, nightmares can be a means by which our unconscious reveals fears and worries that we have been trying to suppress.

WHO IS IN OUR NIGHTMARES?

Now *this* is something I bet you had never thought about: You know those creepy and slimy monsters that chase you in your nightmares? Or those wild animals that lick their chops at the thought of having you for a nice Sunday dinner? Have you ever wondered who they might be? Guess what? They just might be you!

Many dream researchers believe those scary characters in our nightmares may actually represent aspects of ourselves that we don't like very much. That wild and ravenous lion might actually symbolize your ruthless side. Or that snapping alligator might represent your tendency to snap at others when things are bothering you.

When you awaken from a nightmare, try to think metaphorically about who and what was in your dream. As the saying goes, you can run, but you can't hide—not from yourself, at least!

LUCID DREAMS

Lucid dreams are some of my favorites. Have you ever had one of those dreams in which all of a sudden everything seems a little *too* weird, and you stop and say to yourself, "This can't really be happening. I must be dreaming."

Well, if you have had that happen, you've had a lucid dream. Lucid dreams generally start out like other dreams. Then suddenly, something makes you realize you're dreaming. It's sort of like you're half dreaming and half awake.

Like nightmares, lucid dreams are thought to emerge

A dream that is not understood is like a letter not opened.

The Talmud

51

Dreams are the facts from which we must proceed.

Carl Jung

from your unconscious and can reflect a situation in your life that needs to be resolved. But lucid dreams are more accessible to you than nightmares because you actually have the power to control what goes on in the dream.

Researchers have discovered that by participating in your lucid dreams, you can find the answer to problems that you struggle with in your waking life. For example, a friend of mine named Timothy was recently hired as an editorial assistant for a successful publishing house. He was excited and eager to please. In his interview, he had agreed to work for three different editors. He knew that he would need to be more responsible and organized than he had ever been before. After a few months of working for the company, Timothy began to have dreams involving his bosses and his assignments.

In one such dream, he was sitting in his cubicle. Manuscripts, blueprints, layouts, calendars, and disks were piled up so high around him that he couldn't see any way out. He could hear his bosses discussing his deadlines, but could not see them. Suddenly,

Timothy realized that he must be dreaming—there was no way he could really be physically trapped in the cubicle by this much work. He was having a lucid dream. In his dream, he began to move the piles of work to the adjoining (and empty) cubicle. When he could finally see out, his bosses were no longer there; they had left work for the day. Timothy drafted a note to all three of them and left copies of the note on each of their desks before he, too, went home. In his note, he explained that he was enjoying working with each of them but felt overwhelmed.

When Timothy awoke the next morning, he felt an enormous sense of relief. He realized that he needed to talk to his bosses about his workload and the demands of working for three people. That morning, Timothy asked to meet with one of his bosses. He explained his concern to her, and she was very understanding. She then spoke with his other two supervisors, and they agreed that it would be necessary to hire another assistant. They commended Timothy on his effort and his honesty. After Timothy faced his fears, he found working for the publishing house much more enjoyable. Later that year, he got his first promotion!

A dream that is not understood remains a mere occurrence; understood, it becomes a living experience.

Carl Jung

> *The spirit of man has two dwelling places: both this world and the other world. The borderland between them is the third, the land of dreams.*
>
> Bruhad Aranyaka
> *Upanishad*

TAKING CHARGE OF YOUR LUCID DREAMS

Most people have had at least one lucid dream in their lifetime. Some people, however, have them almost nightly. It seems that the more you think about your lucid dreams and prepare for them, the more lucid dreams you will have.

Some dream researchers advise reminding yourself throughout the day that you will have a lucid dream when you go to sleep that night. Other researchers suggest thinking of a problem or situation you would like to confront in your dream. As you begin to drift off to sleep, think about that situation while reminding yourself *you will be in control, you will be in control, you will be in control. . . .*

PARANORMAL DREAMS

Now we have taken a look at nightmares, night terrors, and lucid dreams. All three of these types of dreams have been subject to extensive scientific research. Paranormal dreams, however, are not as easy to examine under a scientific lens. These dreams deal with a person's extrasensory perception (ESP).

A series of experiments by dream researchers Montague Ullman and Stanley Krippner seem to prove that paranormal dreams are possible. In these experiments (which were conducted in the 1960s and '70s at Maimonides Medical Center in Brooklyn, New York), one person–the "sender"–would try to project the image of a certain picture to another person–the "subject"–who was sleeping in another room. The subject was not told what the picture would be; after REM sleep was over, the subject was awakened up and asked to describe his or her dream. These experiments produced quite a few "hits": some of the subjects described dreams that clearly corresponded to the picture being mentally transmitted. But no other scientific researchers have been able to replicate the results of these experiments.

Do you believe in paranormal dreams? Maybe you've had one. See if you've had any of the following types of paranormal dreams. . .

Clairvoyant dreams are dreams in which a person identifies the whereabouts of an object or person, or discerns other factual information, through ESP. For example, say Theresa has lost the key to her diary. She has a dream one night that the key is lodged between her night table and her mattress. The next morning, she looks in this spot and finds the key exactly where she dreamt it would be. However, it is difficult to say, based on Theresa's dream, whether she had made use of ESP or if she had simply reconstructed the day's events (including the key ending up where it did) while sleeping. Do you see why it is often difficult to prove with certainty that a dream was paranormal?

Telepathic dreams are those in which two people communicate in their dreams. The following is an example of two friends having telepathic dreams.

If a little dreaming is dangerous, the cure for it is not to dream less but to dream more, to dream all the time.

Marcel Proust,
Remembrance of Things Past, vol. 4

> **D**reaming permits each and every one of us to be quietly and safely insane every night of our lives.

William Dement, sleep and dream researcher, coined the term "REM" sleep.

Atif was getting ready to take a vacation; he asked his friend Shana to take care of his cat, Simone, while he was gone. Shana had never had a pet before and was very excited by the idea of caring for Simone.

A few days before Atif was scheduled to leave town he had a dream. Although he had been to Shana's apartment only a few times, he dreamt of her apartment in vivid detail. In his dream, he was sitting on the living room couch while Shana was in the kitchen. He was looking at a magazine when he heard a crash outside. Atif turned to look out the window and realized it was wide open. A moment later, another crash woke him up, but it was only Simone knocking over a glass.

Atif wondered what his dream could have meant. He'd been thinking about it all morning when something suddenly clicked: He realized Simone could jump out of Shana's window to the street below and be hit by a car! At that very moment, Shana called Atif on the phone. She asked if she should take any precautions while Simone stayed with her. She said she dreamt the night before that Simone had escaped out a window.

This example demonstrates one theory about telepathic dreams: they can alert two people who are close to each other of a potential problem, conflict, or disaster.

Precognitive dreams are another class of paranormal dreams. Have you ever had the feeling that you've been somewhere before? Or have you ever met someone whom you could swear you've met before, but you can't figure out where or when? If so, you have experienced déjà vu. Some researchers contend that precognitive dreams are responsible for feelings of déjà vu.

Some paranormal dream specialists from the Jungian school believe that we dream of events before they actually happen. Only when the event occurs do we realize we've had a precognitive dream.

The final type of paranormal dream we will look at is the prophetic dream. The prophetic dream is like

I do not know whether I was then a man dreaming I was a butterfly, or whether I am now a butterfly dreaming I am a man.

Chuang-tzu, *On Leveling All Things*

*F*or the
waking
there is one
common
world only.
But when
asleep, each
man turns to
his own pri-
vate world.

Heraclitus, 6th
century B.C.
Greek philosopher

a precognitive dream, except the dreamer (or an interpreter) realizes that the dream is a prediction of future events. One of the best known prophetic dreams is the biblical story of Joseph and the famine in Egypt.

An Egyptian pharaoh had a dream in which he envisioned seven fat cows and seven lean ones. The pharaoh went to Joseph and asked him for his interpretation. Joseph interpreted this dream to mean that Egypt would have seven prosperous years (the seven fat cows) and then seven years of famine (the seven lean cows). Joseph's prophecy resulted in the pharaoh going to great lengths to put aside food and drink in case the famine should truly occur. As it turned out, Joseph was right in his prediction. There were seven years of abundant crops in Egypt, followed immediately by seven barren years. (And Joseph was greatly rewarded for his accurate interpretation of the pharaoh's prophetic dream!)

As with a precognitive dream, one can never be sure if a prophetic dream is accurate or not, until the events in the dream happen or fail to happen.

The waking have one world in common; sleepers have each a private world of his own.

Heraclitus,
Fragments

One word of advice: Don't spend too much of your time dwelling on the negative predictions in prophetic dreams, since they may not come true. Be open-minded and who knows what you will foresee for yourself.

Oh, How I Dreamt of Things Impossible, William Blake

Chapter Four

Dream
Analysis

CHAPTER FOUR:

DREAM ANALYSIS

Not all dreams are hard to figure out. The meanings of some dreams are obvious and some may simply be a rehashing of the day's events and nothing more. Other dreams, however, are not as easy to figure out. They may offer clues into thoughts and feelings you have buried deep in your unconscious. This chapter will help you uncover the mysteries hidden in such dreams. You will learn the following:

* how to remember your dreams
* how to keep a dream journal
* how to interpret your dreams

DREAM RECALL

Some people claim that they never dream, but the truth is everyone dreams. In fact, a person has a few different dreams each night, though usually only the last dream can be remembered. Here are three tips for improving dream recall:

1) Relax—rid your mind of all worry and stress when you get into bed.

2) As you drift off to sleep, tell yourself over and over again, "Tonight I will dream. When I wake up, I will remember what I have dreamt."

3) Try to ensure that you get enough sleep without any interruptions. Disconnect the telephone. If you don't need an alarm clock to wake up, don't use one.

KEEPING A DREAM JOURNAL

This is a must: You will need a dream journal. You can use a fancy journal or a plain notebook. The only requirements for your dream journal are that it is bound (let's try to stay organized here) and that there is plenty of room to write. (If you want Snoopy on the cover, feel free to indulge yourself.) Your journal should be kept close to your bed so that you can grab it as soon as you wake up. Also, keep a pen or pencil with your journal. The memory of most dreams fades shortly after you awaken, so the sooner you start writing down the details of your dream, the better.

In dreams we catch glimpses of a life larger than our own.

Helen Keller

69

We live
as we dream—
alone.

Joseph Conrad,
Heart of Darkness

You're not done preparing just yet! You've got the paper and the pen. But what are you using them for exactly? Let's get those pages set up. Before you go to bed, make sure you have the following information in your journal:

Date: Write the date at the top of the page.

Events of the day: Here you will jot down events of the day that you think may have affected your mood and thoughts, such as "Got a raise!" or "Watched Sammy Sosa hit his 60th homerun!" or "Ate an entire box of bonbons!" See if any of these events occur in your dream.

Questions/Concerns: This is where you can write down any questions or concerns you hope to resolve in your dreams. For example, you may wonder if your significant other could be "the one." Or you are trying to figure out why a coworker seems to have it in for you.

Then, leave room to record your dream(s), and try to get a good night's sleep.

UPON WAKING

As soon as you wake up, whether it's in the middle of the night or early in the morning, grab your journal and start writing. Write anything and everything you can remember about your dream: colors you saw, sounds you heard, people with whom you interacted, conversations, etc. Get down every detail. Even if something seems irrelevant, write it down!

Once you've finished writing down what you can remember about the dream, assess how the dream made you feel. Did you feel anxious when you woke up? Did you feel scared in your dream? Angry? Happy?

Now, you need to reexamine your dream. Let's talk about how to do that.

Tell me not, in mournful numbers, Life is but an empty dream! For the soul is dead that slumbers, And things are not what they seem.

Henry Wadsworth Longfellow, "A Psalm of Life"

IN YOUR DREAMS

Ask yourself the following questions (in this order)
as you go over your notes, then write down your
answers.

* What was my first impression about the dream and
what it could have meant?

* How do I feel about what I dreamt? What mood
was I in during the dream and when I woke up?

* Where and when were events in the dream taking
place?

* Was I in my dream?

* Who was with me in the dream?

* Were there any predominant images or symbols in
the dream (e.g., a dove, rainbow, etc.)?

THE INTERPRETATION

Now that you have all your notes in front of you,
it's time to make sense out of them. Your first
impressions are important—they are your gut reaction

*T*hose
things that
have occupied
a man's
thoughts and
affections
while awake
recur to his
imagination
while asleep.

St. Thomas Aquinas

73

Sender of
true oracles,
While I sleep
send me your
unerring skill
To read what
is and what
will be.

From a Greek
magical papyrus

to the dream and give you a basis from which to proceed in your dream analysis.

Contemplating how you felt in the dream and your response to the dream can provide considerable insight into what your unconscious is trying to tell you. For example, should you awaken in a melancholy mood, it may be that, unconsciously, you feel sad about something even though, on a conscious level, you aren't aware of such feelings.

Where and when the events in your dream took place will help you identify what period of your life your unconscious is referring to as it attempts to resolve something. Let's say that when you were six years old you were at your best friend's birthday party and in the middle of the festivities, she told you that she now had a new best friend. Now, you have a dream that you are at that same birthday party—an event you haven't thought about for over twenty years. Why would you think about it now? It could well be that your mind is associating something with that party and the rejection you felt at the time. Perhaps you are worried that someone you

One of the characteristics of the dream is that nothing surprises us in it. With no regret, we agree to live in it with strangers, completely cut off from our habits and friends.

Jean Cocteau, French author and filmmaker

are close to is trying to push you away. Allow your mind to make free associations—this will help you determine what your dreams are telling you.

Who was with you in the dream? Ask yourself what the characters in your dream were like and if they were similar to you in any way. If one of the characters was an injured man, do you feel that you can relate to him? Are you injured literally or figuratively? If there was a little girl throwing a temper tantrum in your dream, can you relate to her behavior? If one of the characters was an animal, can you relate to its behavior or any of its characteristics? Do you feel like a dog whose owner forgot to refill the water bowl and is away for the weekend? See what associations you can make. If you are still having trouble figuring out what the characters in your dreams symbolize, consult the dream dictionary in the final chapter of this book.

Finally, let's address the images or symbols that were in your dream. Again, begin by making any free associations that come to mind. What do you feel when you imagine a book with all of its pages torn out? What comes to mind when you envision a clean kitchen sink? Don't go overboard when you think metaphorically—your associations should make *some* sense. Once you have come to your own conclusions, you may refer to the dream dictionary and see if your interpretations match those of dream-analysis experts. But remember, your personal insights are more important than the experts' interpretation.

Now, study the notes you have taken on your dream. Put together all the insights you have gained and see what you discover about yourself.

*I*f a man, sitting all alone, cannot dream strange things, and make them look like truth, he need never try to write romances.

Nathaniel Hawthorne, *The Scarlet Letter*

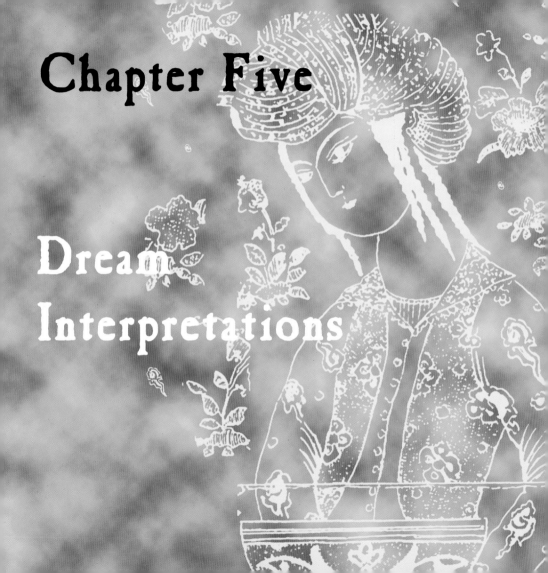

Chapter Five

Dream Interpretations

CHAPTER FIVE:

DREAM INTER-PRETATIONS

In this chapter, you will have a chance to see how six different dreams can be interpreted. For most of these dreams, you will see the dreamer's actual journal entry followed by a step-by-step analysis. After reading these passages you will be better prepared to interpret dreams on your own.

JIM'S DREAM

Date: June 19, 1999

Today: Nothing out of the ordinary happened. Paid a few bills, worked a double shift at the restaurant, stopped by Josh's party for an hour or so, got home really late.

Questions/ Concerns: Too tired to think of any right now!

Dream notes: I'm running up and down city streets and feel anxious. I don't know what I'm running from. Suddenly, I run into a building. I don't know what kind of building it is, so I have no idea why I decided to go in. I enter a huge room. There are rows and rows of seats, and there's an altar at the front. I feel drawn to the altar; yet for some reason, I'm hesitant to approach it. I run for a few minutes through the room. It feels safe because I realize it's a church. There are other people milling around. One of these people turns around and looks right at me. He has a clown face. He's smiling and his eyes look like painted-on stars. I look around and see that everyone has a clown face. I sprint up the stairs. When I reach the top and look down, I have a full view of the big room filled with clowns. Suddenly I realize that the first clown I saw is running up the stairs after me. I turn and head for a big open doorway. I don't know what was on the other side of the doorway because that's where the dream ended—my alarm clock went off.

Following are Jim's notes:

1) **First impression of dream:** My first impression about this dream was that it was kind of creepy, but also funny—it was like I was in my own bizarre

*I*t is best to treat a dream as one would treat a totally unknown object: one looks at it from all sides, takes it in one's hand, carries it about, has all sorts of ideas and fantasies about it, and talks of it to other people.

Carl Jung

81

action film. I'm confused about why I had this dream. I'm not really sure what any of it means.

2) **How do I feel about the dream?** I thought it was funny, but I do feel a bit anxious about it. Actually, I felt anxious during the whole dream.

3) **Where and when did events in the dream take place?** At first, I was running down those city streets. Then, I was in church. The dream seemed to take place during the present.

4) **Who was with me in the dream?** The only other people in my dream were the clowns.

5) **Images/symbols in the dream:** I think the important symbols in my dream were the altar, clowns, the staircase, and wide, open doorway.

THE INTERPRETATION

1) The altar is a place of sacrifice, but also where

The armored cars of dreams contrived to let us do so many a dangerous thing.

Elizabeth Bishop,
American poet,
"Sleeping Standing Up"

Illustration from *Alice's Adventures in Wonderland*, Sir John Tenniel

one finds refuge. Jim is drawn to the altar, but never approaches it—perhaps because he is not religious. He runs frantically throughout the entire dream, yet he is not sure why he was running.

2) Clowns normally represent one of two things to Jim—happiness (if the clown is funny and entertaining) or foreboding (if the clown is the type from horror flicks). Jim got the impression the clowns were the former type.

3) The staircase is a symbol of ascent and descent. In a larger sense, the ups and downs of one's life.

4) The wide doorway is a certain transition between places, and it is an easy transition because there is nothing to stop him—the doors are open.

After Jim thought about what each of the symbols in his dream could mean, he took another look at his dream and extracted a message from it. He was running—that made him think of his job and how busy he's been waiting tables and tending bar. He works so much that he has little time to himself or to spend with

> *A sweet thing, for whatever time, to revisit in dreams the dear dead we have lost.*
>
> Euripides, Alcestis

friends. He didn't know why he was running in his dream, so he associated that aimlessness with his work again. Jim was not happy in his job. He was still trying to figure out what he wanted to do with his life. When he reaches the church in his dream and goes inside, it is quiet and peaceful, not loud and hectic like the restaurant. He feels at peace in the church. In the dream, Jim wants to go up to the altar, yet he doesn't approach it. Jim recognizes this as his tendency to avoid looking for a more satisfying job. While he knows he is intelligent and talented, he feels he is too busy working all the time to make a move. However, after seeing the clowns, Jim runs up the stairs—the clown makes him move. Here's where the dream really began to click for Jim.

Jim has always toyed with the idea of working in comedy. He has a wonderful sense of humor. Since the clown makes him run up the stairs, Jim thinks the dream is a sign that pursuing a career in comedy would be a positive step. Once Jim reaches the top of the stairs, he leaves all the other clowns down below. Jim interprets them as being other aspiring entertainers, whom he surpasses. Jim thinks the clown chasing him through the open doorway might be his ambition spurring him on to a new phase in his life. Of course, Jim woke up before he saw what was on the other side of the doorway (whether success awaits him or not), but that can only be revealed in his waking life. The dream motivated Jim to quit his job and pursue a career in comedy. He has since made many important contacts and gotten a few gigs. He now feels much more at peace with himself.

MARYBETH'S DREAM

Date: April 4, 1998

Today: Went jogging in the park, did laundry, caught up on my magazines, read the paper, watched *Days of Wine and Roses*, ordered in Chinese food.

Question: Although my day was relaxing, why am I feeling so nervous lately?

Dream notes: I'm driving my car through flooded streets.

There's a long, long trail awinding Into the land of my dreams.

Stoddard King, songwriter

Fairies Looking Through an Open Window,
John Anster Christian Fitzgerald

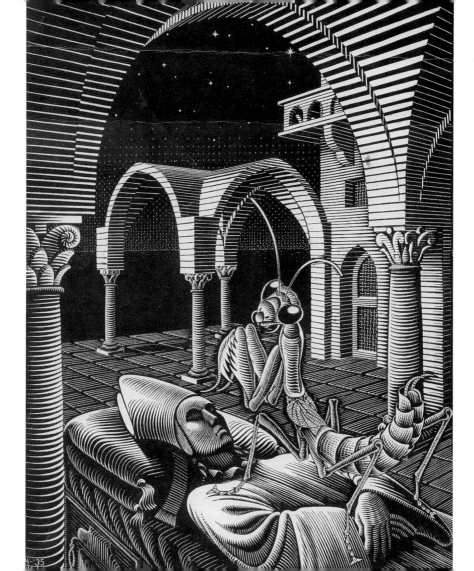

The only other cars on the road are abandoned. I'm very anxious about the road conditions and am clutching the steering wheel tightly. All of a sudden, the car won't turn in the direction I'm steering and the brakes stop working. The car just keeps moving forward. It finally stops. I'm relieved to find a phone and hurriedly begin calling someone—I don't know who—to ask for help. When I get to the last digit, I inadvertently press the wrong number and have to begin dialing all over again. Although I concentrate on the numbers, I just make this same mistake over and over again.

1) **First impression of dream:** I'm frustrated that I can't do something even though I keep trying and trying. That's how I've been feeling lately, in general.

2) **How do I feel about the dream?** The dream left me feeling annoyed and frustrated. It made me feel a little ashamed, too, as if I can't do things right no matter how hard I try.

Whither is fled the visionary gleam? Where is it now, the glory and the dream?

William Wordsworth, "Intimations of Immortality"

> *I* slept and dreamed that life was beauty, I woke—and found that life was duty.

Ellen Strugis Hooper, "Beauty and Day"

3) **Where and when did events in the dream take place?** In my car driving through flooded streets, then at a payphone on a corner. The dream took place during the daytime.

4) **Who was with me in the dream?** No one. I was all alone.

5) **Images/symbols in the dream:** flooded streets, abandoned cars, steering wheel, brakes, and pay phone.

THE INTERPRETATION

1) The flooded streets symbolize danger. They made it difficult for Marybeth to get where she was going.

2) Abandoned cars made Marybeth feel alone on the road, as if other people had decided not to face the same treacherous roads that she was on.

The Captive Robin, Richard Doyle

3) The steering wheel was her means of having control over where she went.

4) The loss of brakes was like a loss of control.

5) The pay phone was a way to communicate and get help, but she never connected with anyone.

With all this insight, Marybeth began to make big strides in her interpretation. She realized that this dream paralleled how she had been feeling lately about life in general. In the dream, Marybeth was trying to navigate her way through a scary situation, but she felt like she had no control over it. She feels alone in the dream. Finally, she finds a means by which she can reach out to someone (the phone) but when she tries, it's impossible. It's her fault that she can't find anyone to help because she keeps making an error when dialing the number. Marybeth saw many connections to her real life. She had just moved to a big city after a divorce. She felt scared being on her own for the first time in years. Everything was so expensive and she just couldn't seem to budget correctly. Her apartment was in a large building, but she hadn't really made any

*D*reams are an involuntary kind of poetry.

Jean Paul Richter, German novelist of the nineteenth century

Naughty Josephina Lara, Guadalupe Posada

*D*reams are often most pro- found when they seem most crazy.

Sigmund Freud, *The Interpretation of Dreams*

friends yet. She had been invited to a party at one neighbor's place, but could not attend. Marybeth realized that her failure to make connections with other people had left her feeling frustrated and alone.

Soon after the dream, she made an effort to get together with the neighbor who had invited her over. They became good friends and, through her, Marybeth was introduced to other people she liked very much. Within months, Marybeth realized that she liked her newfound independence and was happier than she had been in a long time.

ERIN'S DREAM

Date: October 14, 1999

Today: Bad day at work! Going crazy there. Starting to hate my boss. He doesn't appreciate all my hard work. He only favors employees who kiss up to him.

Question: Is it time for me to move on and find a new job?

Dream notes: I was on line at a deli, trying to get my lunch. It was one of those places where you take a number, so I did. I really wanted pasta salad. I kept staring at the pasta salad, wanting it more and more, but the counter person wouldn't take my order, even though it was my turn. He just kept going to the next person. Everyone else was getting the pasta salad, so I just kept watching it get smaller and smaller. And I never got any.

1) **First impression of the dream:** I think the dream parallels my situation at work and the frustration I feel.

2) **How do I feel about the dream?** Frustrated and angry.

3) **Where and when did events in the dream take place?** In a deli, at lunch time.

4) **Who was with me in the dream?** The other customers and the deli worker who refused to wait on me.

*I*t is not our idleness, in our dreams, that the submerged truth some-times comes to the top.

Virginia Woolf

> Our conscious minds are needed if we are to make the most of our dreams; by bringing them into waking consciousness and learning to understand them we may be led to a reappraisal of our whole mode of being.
>
> Ann Faraday, *Dream Power*

5) **Images/symbols in the dream:** The deli, the pasta salad, the mean deli worker, the other customers.

THE INTERPRETATION

Erin's dream was not too difficult for her to decipher. She came to the following conclusion: The deli was her office. The deli worker was her boss. Just as she felt unappreciated at work, the deli worker was ignoring her. The pasta salad, in Erin's opinion, represented the recognition she deserved. Watching the other customers—whom she took to be her co-workers—get their recognition, while she still waited for hers, was driving her mad. Erin saw this dream as a message that she was not being treated fairly at work and, as a result, her self-esteem was suffering. She decided to meet with an employment agent, and soon went on to land a new job where she is very much appreciated.

CLAIRE'S DREAM

Date: October 25, 1999

Today: Busy day at the office. Made dinner for Tom. Had hoped to have a romantic evening, but Tom got home later than he expected. He was very apologetic, but I couldn't help feeling annoyed. We watched a video, but I fell asleep within 30 minutes. So much for my plans for a romantic evening!

Questions/Concerns: Am I feeling satisfied in my marriage? Am I being too sensitive? Why am I feeling as if everything Tom does is wrong lately?

Dream notes: I'm in a two-story house, struggling to lead a horse up the stairs. The horse is calm and willing to follow me but, as you can imagine, it's not easy leading a horse up the stairs of a house. I'm walking along beside, then in front of, the horse, holding the reins. There's

*T*he dream ...is a texture woven of time and space inside which we find ourselves.

Robert Bosnack

99

barely enough room for me in the stairwell, and I'm sort of pushed up against the wall—especially when it comes to turns on the stairs. In the dream, I had the sense that the house belonged to friends of mine (though their real house is nothing like the one in the dream).

1) **First impression of dream:** I felt really frustrated in my dream. The dream annoyed me, because I was insisting on trying to get that huge horse up the stairs with me, even though I knew it was pretty much impossible.

2) **How do I feel about the dream?** I felt put out and discouraged. I was upset with my situation and my persistence. I really wanted to just let go of the horse's reins and walk away, but something wouldn't let me.

3) **Where and when did events in the dream take place?** They all took place in a two-story house

*R*eally become the thing—whatever it is in a dream—become it.... Lose your mind and come to your senses.

Frederick S. Perls, psychotherapist

101

Advice from a Caterpillar, Arthur Rackham

> **O**God, I
> could be
> bounded in a
> nutshell and
> count myself a
> king of infi-
> nite space,
> were it not
> that I have bad
> dreams.
>
> William Shakespeare,
> *Hamlet*

that belonged to a couple I feel very close to. The house, although it was theirs in my dream, in no way resembled their real house. Their real house is only one story.

4) **Who was with me in the dream?** Just me and that monster of a horse!

5) **Images/symbols in the dream:** The images and symbols that felt important to me were the horse, the reins, the stairwell, and the many turns on the stairs that I was forced to make.

THE INTERPRETATION

1) Dreams that feature horses are most frequently associated with the dreamer's love life. Claire's perception of the horse was that it was quite a nuisance to her and prevented her from getting where she wanted to go (in this particular instance, she wanted to climb the stairs). As we continue, we begin to see a parallel between her struggle with

the horse and her current experiences with her husband. The horse therefore represents her husband.

2) Ascending a staircase signifies a path to personal success. It seems as if Claire is desperate to attain success. However, the horse—her husband—is making this ascent exhausting and difficult for her.

3) The fact that Claire has the reins of the horse may very well symbolize her need to control the relationship. However, having the reins is still not affording her all of the control that she needs.

4) The twists and turns in the staircase simply reconfirm her struggle. It is at these points in her ascent that she feels most hindered. She has no control over the design of the stairwell, and gets discouraged.

Claire's dream and its meaning became very clear to her. With Tom so busy due to his business taking off, they had been losing touch with each other. She misses spending time with him. Despite her desperate attempts to recreate the past, outside forces are working against them.

For in that sleep of death what dreams may come.

William Shakespeare
Hamlet

Claire had little trouble figuring out why the dream had taken place at her friends' house. This particular couple was one that Claire had recently begun to resent. They seemed to have the perfect marriage. This dream was bringing to light the jealousy she felt toward them and their marital bliss.

By trying to lead the horse (her husband) up the stairs, Claire was trying to keep their marriage alive. She felt that she was responsible for rekindling their romance; hence, her hold of the reins. However, the horse was not cooperating. Claire took this to mean that Tom's newfound success in his work was putting a strain on their marriage.

After this dream, Claire resolved to speak with Tom about how she was feeling. She realized that communication and compromise were in order. She and Tom resolved to keep at least two evenings a week free so they could spend more time with each other. Since then, their marriage has improved.

The time-less in you is aware of life's timelessness; and knows that yesterday is but today's memory and tomorrow is today's dream.

Kahlil Gibran

AMY'S DREAM

Date: December 1, 1995

Today: Went to work. Same old routine. Met some of my girlfriends for happy hour at a nearby bar. Probably had one too many. While my friends all headed home to their husbands or boyfriends, I rode the subway home to my empty apartment, feeling sort of depressed because I have no significant other. Had two big bowls of ice cream (which I did NOT need), and now I feel even worse. Am going to sleep.

Questions/Concerns: Why do I feel so sad? If I were in a relationship right now, would I still feel so down in the dumps?

Dream notes: I am at home. A hurricane is raging outside. There is no electricity, and the eye of the storm is hitting my area. I feel a sense of urgency and am very nervous because of the storm. The next thing I know, my younger sister is with me. She and I go from room to room, making sure the windows are securely closed and nothing has been damaged by the storm. Oddly enough, an old picture of one of my ex-boyfriends is on my bedside table, and it is one of the first things I check on. Then, I look out a window and see that the streets are becoming flooded. Curious to see how close the water has come to my building, I go outside. The water is now raging in circles like a whirlpool. Even though I'm very scared, I feel compelled to move closer to the water to see how strong the whirlpool is. Then, I chicken out: I decide the situation is too dangerous, so I stop. Suddenly, I'm in my college fiction-writing class and my teacher is reminding us that our short story is due the next day, and he will accept no excuses for tardiness and will grant no extensions. I start to panic because I've only written a few pages, and I have a final exam in biology the next day as well. After class, I tell my friends that I'm dropping the writing course.

Dreams are true while they last and do we not live in dreams?

Alfred, Lord Tennyson

1) **First impression of dream:** Upon waking up from this dream, I feel incredibly stressed. I feel like my mind won't give me a break even when I'm asleep. Everything that plagues my mind throughout the day spills over into my sleep now, too.

2) **How do I feel about the dream?** I feel as if I'm a weak character and a quitter in my dream. I want to get close to the water, but I'm afraid of it. Then, I fail to do my writing assignment, so I decide to walk away from the course entirely.

3) **Where and when did events in the dream take place?** First I was in my apartment. It felt as if I was in the present. Then I moved outside. Before I knew it, I was back in the past, in one of my college classrooms.

4) **Who was with me in the dream?** In the beginning of my dream, I was alone. Then my sister

The eye of man hath not heard, the ear of man hath not seen, man's hand is not able to taste, his tongue to conceive, nor his heart to report what my dream was.

Bottom in William Shakespeare's *A Midsummer Night's Dream*

Dreams, Thomas Nast

I arise from dreams of thee In the first sweet sleep of night, When the winds are breathing low, And the stars are shining bright.

Percy Bysshe Shelley, "The Indian Serenade"

appeared to help me. In the end, I was in a classroom with classmates and my writing professor.

5) **Images/symbols in the dream:** windows, hurricane, raging water, a whirlpool, my ex-boyfriend's picture, a teacher, an exam.

THE INTERPRETATION

The dream was stressful. Not coincidentally, Amy's life was full of stress when she had the dream. Every time water is depicted in her dream, it is dangerous. Hurricanes, floods, whirlpools—they all show Amy's feeling that her life is out of her control.

As we can tell from Amy's notes about the day before she had this dream, she was not getting very much satisfaction from her job and was feeling lonely. She noted that it bothered her that her girlfriends all had men waiting for them. Unlike them, Amy returned home alone, and this seemed to increase her depression. She then ate some ice cream, which she regretted and which made her feel even worse about herself.

In fact, Amy had been struggling with loneliness for over a year. Even her kid sister had a new boyfriend. For the past few months, Amy had been drowning her loneliness in bars, with co-workers and friends. But this was not making her feel better—in fact, it often made her feel worse. Deep down, she never felt truly satisfied—even when she should have been having a great time. First and foremost, she wanted to be in love and couldn't figure out what it would take for her to find the right person. It was especially frustrating that everyone else she knew seemed to have no such problem.

Amy knows that she is shy. She has difficulty opening up to strangers and would be too embarrassed to admit to her friends that she was lonely. In fact, she did such a good job pretending she was happy with her independence that even her closest friends never suspected that she did not like being alone. To make things worse, in social situations, Amy concentrated wholeheartedly on those she knew well and thus, she rarely made new acquaintances.

Always dream and shoot higher than you know how to. Don't bother just to be better than your contemporaries or predecessors. Try to be better than yourself.

William Faulkner

111

This dream made many things clear to Amy. She felt there might be impending danger in her life, and she did not feel safe and secure by herself. When her sister appeared to help her make sure everything was okay, the first thing Amy checked on was a photograph of her ex-boyfriend. (She hadn't thought of him in years!) As scared as Amy felt in the dream, she knew she had to go outside and face her fears (which, in her dream, was the raging water). However, she turned back when the danger seemed great and never allowed herself to find out what would happen if she faced her fears straight on. Instead, she found herself back in her past (in the writing course), feeling like a quitter.

Amy decided it was time to change: she no longer wanted to quit when the going got a little tough. Amy started thinking about her ex-boyfriend and wondered why she had dreamt about him. She was curious if he was married by now, or if he had moved away. She checked the phone book and saw he was still listed. At first she couldn't muster up the courage to call, and for the next couple of days, she ran through a series of imagined conversations.

*I*t may be that those who do most, dream most.

Stephen Locke

113

Finally, a few days later, after practicing what she would say, she called him. The conversation was friendly, and Amy found out he was still single.

They met for dinner and dated again a couple of times. As it turned out, it didn't take Amy very long to remember why they had broken up. However, taking the initiative in this relationship gave Amy the confidence to reach out more openly to other people—and to make an effort to meet new people more readily.

So, as in this case, dreams can sometimes shed light on things you are reluctant to do. The dream made Amy realize she didn't want to quit dating and end up alone, simply because she was scared of getting back out there and looking for Mr. Right. Amy is now much happier with her love life and life in general.

Was it a vision, or a waking dream? Fled is that music: —Do I wake or sleep?

John Keats, "Ode to a Nightingale"

115

Trust in dreams, for in them is hidden the gate to eternity.

Kahlil Gibran

A RECURRING DREAM AND IT'S MESSAGE

For this dream, I have no journal entry. This was a dream my mother told me about when she found out I was going to write this book. She wrote a passage for me, and it reads as follows:

For several weeks in college, I had a recurring dream that really disturbed me. At least two or three times a week, I would dream that I was at a crowded party when I suddenly had the sensation that my legs were giving out beneath me. In each dream, I would try to leave the party discreetly so no one would notice that I couldn't walk. In one variation of the dream, I would be trying to climb a flight of stairs on all fours while people hovered about me trying to help. I just wanted to be left alone: for some reason, I found my inability to walk very embarrassing. In another version of the dream, I would escape from the party through a door to a garden and crawl across the grass. Again, people would be all over me, trying to help.

Fairies Whirl, Arthur J. Black

I 'll let you be in my dream if I can be in yours.

Bob Dylan

I wondered if this dream meant I had some deep-seated fear of being crippled, or if I was developing some phobia about being in crowds, or if I felt that, living in a dormitory, there were too many people hovering about. Then, while napping one afternoon, I found myself in the middle of this very dream when a friend knocked on my door to say I had a phone call. When I tried to get up, I collapsed. My legs had "fallen asleep" while I was napping. I realized that rather than awaken, I just worked my crampy legs into my dream. After that discovery I was occasionally awakened by my bad circulation, but I never had that dream again.

My mother's dream is an example of a recurring dream. Just like any dream, recurring dreams have a message for us, and they may continue to recur until you correctly interpret the dream's message. In this case, my mother had not yet realized on a conscious level that her circulation was poor and that she lost feeling in her legs when she slept–a physical problem that was incorporated into her dream. It is important to be aware that your body can reveal something about your health while you are sleeping.

I hope you found these sample dream interpretations helpful to you in analyzing your own dreams. Still stumped on what something in your dream might mean? Check out the dream dictionary in the next chapter.

To all, to each, a fair goodnight, And pleasing dreams, and slumbers light!

Sir Walter Scott, "Marmion, L'Envoy"

Chapter Six

ream

ictionary

The following is a dream dictionary, with over 200 images and symbols that often appear in dreams and what experts believe they represent. Keep in mind that an image can symbolize different things to different people. Use the list of interpretations as a guide, but look at your own life and trust your gut feelings when trying to figure out the symbols in your dreams.

DREAM DICTIONARY

ABUSE

If you are the abuser in the dream, you may feel guilty about the way you are treating someone. If you are being abused in the dream, you may feel victimized by someone.

ACCIDENT

This may be a precognitive dream; be extra careful when driving or performing an activity in which accidents are more likely to occur.

ADOPTION

You may feel confused about your identity.

ADULTERY

You may have suspicions about your partner's fidelity, or you may want to act out a forbidden temptation—sexual or otherwise. According to Freud, dreams about adultery are a means by which you can safely fulfill your wishes without having to deal with the repercussions.

ADVANCEMENT

A good omen; deep down, you are aware that good fortune is coming.

AIRPLANE

If you are a passenger on an airplane, it means you feel that your life is changing. If you are watching an airplane disappear in the dream, it symbolizes that you have avoided a conflict.

ALARM

You have reason to be worried. Your unconscious is telling you a disaster could occur. (Or maybe your alarm clock is going off!)

ALLEY

You feel as if you are lost, or that your path in life lacks focus. However, if the alley is lit, it means that you have found a unique way of accomplishing things in your life.

ALMANAC

You may be preoccupied with meaningless details in your life.

AMBULANCE

Be wary—ambulances with sirens are bad omens. If you are on board the ambulance, it could mean you will suffer an accident or serious illness.

AMPUTATION

You are experiencing some sort of loss in your life.

AMUSEMENT PARK

Pleasure and merriment. Either you are currently happy with your life, or you can soon expect a period of mirth.

ANCHOR

You are either seeking stability or you feel that someone or something is weighing you down. You may be in a relationship with a person who is too needy.

ANGEL

You feel safe, you trust your instincts, or you believe someone is watching over you. Enjoy this comfortable feeling.

ANTENNAE

You feel distrustful of a relationship you are in. Your unconscious is telling you that you need to examine this relation

ship and evaluate its effect on you. Be forewarned!

APPLES

Good health. You feel healthy, physically and/or mentally.

ARCH

Success. You are accom-

plishing or will accomplish a great feat.

ARROW

Fortune and pleasure. However, if the arrow is broken, you can expect difficulty and obstacles in your path.

ASHES

Failure. You may feel that you have failed at something, or that other people are failing you.

ASYLUM

Mental anguish or a feeling of being overwhelmed. It is time to reprioritize and simplify your life

ATTIC

Imagine that a house is the body; the attic is the head. Attics represent delusion. You believe the impossible can happen. Whatever fancy ideas you are entertaining won't manifest themselves in reality. So get back down to earth!

AUTOMOBILE

You are pursuing (or traveling toward) a goal. If the trip goes well, your aspirations will come true. If, however, you get into a car accident in the dream, it is a sign that you will probably not reach your goals.

B

BABY

An indication you may be suppressing anxieties about the ticking of your biological clock. You are ready to start a family or you feel the need to nurture someone, even if it's not your own child. It could also mean a project you are working on will soon come to fruition.

BALLOON

Like a real balloon, a balloon in a dream cannot last long. This means you are involved in something that will provide only fleeting pleasure. Beware; just as balloons pop, your hopes, dreams, and expectations may be shattered.

BAPTISM

You are seeking a change, a new beginning. Perhaps it is time to simplify your life.

BARE FEET

You feel unprepared for something that is happening or will soon happen to you; you do not have the necessary skills or tools to accomplish something you are attempting.

BARN

A barn with healthy livestock means you are enjoying or will soon enjoy prosperity. If the barn is empty, expect failure or poverty.

BASKET

An empty basket means your life is not as fulfilling as you would like it to be. But if the basket is full, you most likely find your life satisfying.

BATH

If the bath water is hot in your dream, beware of something evil lurking around the corner. Cold bath water, however, means that joyful news is on its way.

BATS

A bad omen; you will soon experience affliction in your life. White bats symbolize an upcoming death.

BEARD

Expect a major struggle in your life. You may have to compete for something you feel is rightfully yours.

BEES

Profit. Expect increased earnings or professional advancement.

BEGGAR

If you are the beggar, you are feeling as if you will lose everything you value. You must better manage your finances or other areas of your life. On the other hand, if someone is begging from you in the dream, you feel taken advantage of. You must deal with whomever you feel is exploiting you.

BICYCLE

If you are riding a bicycle uphill, it's likely you have been working toward a goal. Riding uphill in dreams is also equated with good fortune, while riding downhill may imply that your life is spinning out of control. Riding your bike on level ground may just mean it's time to exercise!

BINOCULARS

Like antennae, binoculars mean there is someone in your life you distrust and may want to keep a closer eye on.

BIRDS

Good fortune. The more colorful the bird or lovelier its tune, the more good fortune you can expect. If a bird is killed in a dream, it is a sign of bad luck.

BOAT/RAFT

Boating in calm waters is a positive sign; there are good things in store for you. But watch out if the waters in your dream are stormy—a sign that there is trouble ahead.

BOX

If the box is filled, you can expect good things to happen. An empty box is a sign that what you hoped for is not going to materialize.

BOAT'S CABIN

The cabin of a boat is generally associated with trouble. Either you are involved in a dangerous relationship or will soon meet someone who will bring misfortune into your life.

BRIDE

A symbol of union. The union may not necessarily be marital, but will likely be long lasting.

BURGLAR

You are subconsciously aware that something of yours is being sought and may soon be taken from you. You must be vigilant if you wish to maintain what is rightfully yours.

BURIED ALIVE

This means you have made an enormous error, or are about to. Be careful in your decision making.

BUTCHER

You feel as if your character is under scrutiny or is being picked apart; others question your honor or integrity.

BUTTERFLY

Butterflies portend the reappearance of an old friend.

BUZZARD

Scandal. You may be involved in a scandal right now and are more upset by it than you realize. Otherwise, you may soon be a victim of gossip and slander.

C

CAGE

Seeing animals trapped in a cage portends that you will win an important battle. If, however, you are the one trapped inside a cage, you may feel you are losing an important dispute.

CAKE

Satisfaction. You have been indulging yourself and quite enjoy being pampered.

CALENDAR

Keeping your life organized is of great importance to you right now.

CANAL

If the water in the canal is dirty or foul, you may expect a period of sickness. If the water is clear, you can expect good health for the next several years.

CANDLE

If the candle is burning low, it is a sign that you will soon experience a period of great confusion. Putting out a candle in your dreams indicates that you are repressing important thoughts and ideas.

CAROUSEL

Riding on a carousel indicates you are stuck in a very dull routine. However, if you are watching another person ride a carousel, it means that you are feeling envious of someone else.

CAT

Bad luck. Beware of a diabolic stranger who seeks to corrupt your world.

CEMETERY

If the cemetery is well-maintained, it is likely that you will enjoy several years of good heath. But if the cemetery is abandoned or unkempt, expect a period of isolation and unhappiness.

CHILD

A child in a dream often represents the dreamer as a child. You may have some unresolved issues from childhood—the rest of the dream's content will give you clues into what these unresolved issues are.

CLIMBING

The satisfying completion of a hike or climb means you feel proud of a major accomplishment. If, however, you find the climb tiresome, reconsider your expectations—you may have set unrealistic goals.

CLOWN

Happy clowns are associated with joy and merriment while sad ones generally signify defeat. Evil clowns signify deception and trickery. If you are the clown, expect to be ridiculed and mocked by others behind your back.

COFFIN

Almost always associated with death, illness, loneliness, or sorrow.

CRADLE

Rocking a baby in a cradle may seem like a beautiful image to you, but you musn't be fooled. In fact, this may be a premonition that a close family member is seriously ill. Rocking an

empty cradle is also a bad omen: you must beware of gossip and rumors that may lead to your demise.

D

DARKNESS
Indicates that you are intentionally being left out or played for a fool by people who are close to you.

DENTIST
A dentist at work often means you feel uneasy about someone or something.

DEVIL
You feel shame or despair.

DIAMONDS
Almost always an auspicious sign. If, however, the diamonds have been

taken from a deceased person in the dream, your good fortune may just be a sham and you should beware.

DICTIONARY
A sign that you are too dependent on others and what they may think. Take this dream as a cue to seek more autonomy and self-assurance.

DIVORCE
Indicates dissatisfaction in your marriage.

DOOR
Passing through a door means you feel you are being stalked. Someone

else passing through a door means an important endeavor of yours will fail.

DOORKNOCKER

You are in desperate need of the advice or aid of someone close to you. A predicament you thought you could handle on your own is not as simple as you had originally believed.

DOVE

Peace. Perhaps it is time to reconcile with someone with whom you have quarreled.

DRAGON

A symbol of impending chaos. It may be time to organize your life and tie up some loose ends.

DRUM

The muffled sound of a drum is actually the call of an absent friend. Someone with whom you are close but who lives far away is in dire need of your help.

To see, but not hear, a drum is an indication that you will soon reap the just rewards of your good deeds.

E

EATING

If you are dining alone, it is a sign that you are experiencing some sort of difficulty in your social relation- ships. If you are dining with others, your dream denotes a prosperous period in your life–either in the present or near future.

ECHO
Loneliness–others are not responding to you in a positive manner.

EGGS
Many eggs suggest great fortune. However, broken eggs portend an unsuccessful financial investment.

ELEVATOR/ ESCALATOR
If you are ascending in an elevator, you will soon reach great heights in your career. However, if the elevator is descending, it is likely that your career is in a downward phase.

ENVELOPE
Unfortunately, an envelope in a dream portends misfortune. Expect to be disappointed by some news coming your way.

EXPLOSION
Stress–you are anxious about a certain aspect of your life.

EYE
You are suspicious of someone.

F

FAINTING
Strangely enough, fainting in a dream doesn't mean you should be worried about your own health. Rather, fainting often suggests that someone in your family has fallen ill.

FAIRY

A good omen—enjoy!

FALLING

If you land safely from a fall, you will prevail in a struggle. If, however, you injure yourself upon landing, it is likely that you will not achieve victory. Falling can also symbolize insecurity or a surrender to erotic temptation.

FAME

If you dream that you are famous, you will not find the success you have been anticipating. Oddly enough, if you are not the famous person in the dream, you will reach the heights you imagined.

FARM

A prosperous future.

FATHER (OR FATHER FIGURE)

A father figure in a dream may appear as a father, grandfather, or king. He may be protective, or overbearing and destructive. If you dream of being a father figure in the dream, it is a sign that you feel self-assured and in control. If someone else is the father figure, it is a sign that you feel inferior to this person.

FATIGUE

A dream in which you suffer from fatigue may be a sign that you are not well.

FIRE

Dreams of fire are much like dreams of falling. If you are not harmed by the fire, you will emerge safely from a difficult situation. However, if you are burned in the fire, you are concerned about conflicts you are facing.

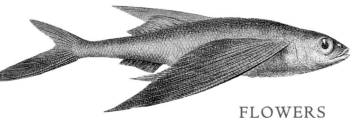

FLYING
You desire freedom; you want to get out of a situation you are in.

FLOWERS
You have or will soon have many admirers. However, if the flowers are wilted, those who used to admire you are losing interest.

FISH
Fish swimming through clear water indicate financial success. Fish swimming in murky water mean you should be cautious with your money.

FLOATING
If you are floating in clear water, you will rise above obstacles in your life. If you are floating in muddy water, you may prevail over obstacles but will not be satisfied with your success.

FOREIGNER
If your encounter with a foreigner is positive, luck is on your side. A negative encounter portends misfortune.

FOUNTAIN

Clear water in a fountain indicates that an intimate relationship is pleasing. Murky water may suggest involvement in a risky love affair.

FUNERAL

Never a good omen. If you are being buried, it is likely that you are unsatisfied in matters of love. If someone else is being buried, you will soon find out that someone close to you has fallen ill.

G

GARDEN

Contentment with your life. If you are strolling through a garden, you can expect that the complacency you are experiencing will last for a long time.

GHOST

Danger; especially if the ghost is of a deceased parent or close friend.

GLOVES

Exercise caution in your financial dealings.

GOGGLES

A key person in your life is trying to manipulate you. Do not allow yourself to be persuaded by those whom you do not fully trust.

GRAVE

A bad omen. Dreaming of a grave is said to precede a major disappointment in your life.

GYPSY

If you dream that a gypsy is reading your palm or telling your future, beware. It means you are about to enter into a marriage or other important union that will be unsuccessful.

H

HAND

If the hand is well-manicured and youthful, look forward to success. If the hand is old and wrinkled, beware of an upcoming financial disaster.

HARP

A period of bliss and merriment will soon come to an end.

HAT

Hats are associated with fortune in the business world. If you are sporting a new hat in your dream, you may be considering a lucrative business deal. If you lose your hat in your dream, it is a sign that you are headed for a work-related disaster.

HELL

Dangerous temptations.

HERMIT

To see a hermit in your dreams indicates that you have been, or will soon be, betrayed by someone close to you. If you, yourself, are the hermit, you have been a good and true friend to others—whether or not they have reciprocated your selflessness.

HERO

If you dream of being a hero, it is a sign that you should "go for it." It is time to take action and pursue your goals.

HOME

A shabby or unkempt home indicates you must take more care of your finances. A house that appears in good condition portends a period of economic comfort.

HORSE

A healthy, well-groomed horse indicates a satisfactory love life. A sick or malnourished horse suggests questions about your partner's fidelity. If a horse should buck you, a rival may be seeking to destroy your love life.

HOSPITAL

If you are in a hospital or infirmary, someone you consider a friend is out to harm you. If you are leaving a hospital, you have escaped (or soon will escape) the clutches of this hurtful person.

I

ICE

A period of distress.

ICE CREAM

A good omen—you will have time to enjoy life's little pleasures.

INCENSE

Friends will be more supportive of you than ever before.

IVY

You will enjoy good health and prosperity.

J

JAIL

If you are the person in jail, you may feel you are unqualified in some area. If another person is in jail, you may feel that someone is taking you for granted.

JEALOUSY

You are jealous of someone you know, though the person in the dream may not be the one you are jealous of.

JOURNEY

If your journey is pleasant, your career is (or soon will be) on track. If the trip is not enjoyable, you may be having job-related problems.

K

KEY

Losing a key suggests domestic turmoil. If you find a key, or keys play a useful role in your dream, you can expect a lengthy period of tranquility in your household.

KISS

The person being kissed is more meaningful to you than you may have realized. If you are not physically attracted to the person you are kissing, you may envy this person or desire to be more like him or her.

KITE

If it is you who are flying the kite, you have been pretentious and a bit of a showoff, of late. Should the kite drop to the ground or become entangled in a tree, you can expect to be knocked off your

The Kiss, Gustav Klimt

high horse. If, however, the kite flies so high that you lose sight of it, pleasant surprises are on the way.

KNIFE

A bad omen. You are or soon will be involved in a major dispute. The larger or rustier the knife is, the more serious the dispute will be.

KNOCKING

You will soon receive unexpected news. The louder the knocking, the more important the news.

L

LADDER

If a ladder is propped up for you to climb, it indicates future success. If you climb down from or fall from a ladder, be prepared for professional disappointment.

LAMP

A brightly lit lamp means you soon will be enlightened about something important. A dim lamp suggests that

loved ones are keeping you in the dark about something significant.

LAUGHING

You are seeking a more eventful social life.

LEAKING

Something of crucial importance to you has been lost.

LEMON

You are envious of someone you recently met.

LEPROSY

You are more upset than you realize about a recent loss.

LIFEBOAT

If you are in a lifeboat, you have given up on something rather than persevere.

LION

You are feeling driven by something forceful—that force is depicted as a lion. If the lion in your dream is in a cage, you must overcome many trials and tribulations in order to achieve the success you seek. Lion cubs signify new undertakings or ventures that will enable you to accomplish the ambitious goals you have set for yourself. A lion's roar portends unexpected advancement in your career.

LIZARD

An enemy is trying everything in his or her power to destroy you. If you manage to destroy the lizard, you will prevail in an upcoming battle. If the lizard remains at large in your dream, it is likely that your enemy will prevail.

LYING

If you are the liar in a dream, you feel guilty about the dishonorable way you have been treating someone.

M

MAP

Indicates that you want to make a significant

change in your life, such as a relocation or change of job.

MASK

Duplicity. If you are wearing a mask in your dream, you may be ashamed of some aspect of your behavior.

MEDICINE

If you take medicine in the dream, a major worry will cease to be a problem for you. If, however, you dispense medicine to another, you do not wish this person well.

MILK

A life of luxury and ease.

MISTLETOE

Portends an enjoyable reunion with a close friend or lover.

MOTHER (OR MOTHER FIGURE)

If there is a maternal figure in the dream, such as a caring mother or grandmother, it is an indication that you feel

safe and protected. However, a negative female figure such as an "evil stepmother" is a sign that someone you thought you could trust is really out to harm you. If you are the mother in the dream, you feel responsible for taking care of others.

MOTORCYCLE
You feel in control of your life, both personally and professionally.

MOUNTAIN
(See *Climbing*.)

MURDER
If you are the victim of a murder, beware of enemies. If you are the murderer in your dream, you probably feel guilty about mistreating a loved one.

N

NEST
A full bird's nest symbolizes a rewarding business matter. An empty nest may symbolize feelings of melancholy about the loss of a close friend or relative.

NIGHTINGALE
A sweetly singing nightingale indicates a peaceful home and a happy marital union.

NUDITY
Embarrassment or a feeling of vulnerability.

O

OAR
Using an oar signifies that you have been sacrificing your own happiness in order to please someone else.

Under the Wave at Kanagawa,
Katsushika Hokusai

OCEAN

A calm ocean indicates a peaceful life. A rough ocean indicates many obstacles to overcome.

ONION

You are envied by many. The more onions in your dream, the more envied you are. If you consume the onions in their entirety, you will be unharmed by those who are jealous of you. If the onions are growing in a garden, you can expect to be challenged by people who are envious of your wealth and happiness. Onions that are cooked portend successful and solid relationships with your coworkers.

ORCHARD

An orchard filled with sweet, ripe fruit signifies a happy love life. If the orchard is barren, or its fruits are out of season, a current relationship will fail.

ORPHAN

A tendency to put the needs of others before your own.

OWL

An owl heard calling in your dreams is believed

to foretell the death of a close friend or relative. If you spot a dead owl in your dream, it means that someone you know who is sick may soon lose his or her battle with the illness. An owl seen but not heard in a tree is a warning—beware the wrath of an enemy.

P

PAIN
There is a need to consult a doctor about your health. If others are in pain, your ability to make decisions may be questionable.

PARACHUTE
A descending parachute signifies a deep desire to abandon something in your life.

PARADISE
If you're dwelling in paradise, you can count on your friends and family. If, however, you are seeking paradise but never find it, it is a sign to be careful when making decisions.

PEACOCK
You are attracted to someone who is not genuine.

PEARLS
Loss of a pearl necklace suggests your success is in jeopardy.

PIANO
Seeing or listening to a piano means you may be about to receive some wonderful news. If, however, the piano is

broken or out of tune, the news will not be so good.

PICKPOCKET
Someone you are close to is not trustworthy.

POISON
If you have been poisoned, someone you consider to be a friend is really duplicitous. If you poison someone, it is a sign you have become jealous of a close friend.

PRIEST
A bad omen. You will soon suffer a humiliation or deception.

RABBIT
A white rabbit is a good omen, signifying a faithful lover or a positive event in the near future.

RACE
Stiff competition. If you win the race, you will surpass any and all

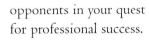

opponents in your quest for professional success.

RAINBOW
A symbol of merriment and joy. Your worries will soon end and your relationships with those close to you will thrive.

RAFT
(See *Boat*.)

RAPIDS
Rapid "white water" signifies an incredibly stressful period in your life. If you are immersed in the rapids, it's a sign that you are in the midst of this stressful period

and should seek help. If you are watching the rapids from a distance, a period of great anxiety may be coming your way.

RAZOR

Expect a major disagreement with a loved one. If the razor cuts skin, an arrangement you made with someone is about to fall through. A razor that is broken or rusty portends distress and disappointment.

RECORD PLAYER

You can expect many years of joy and family harmony.

RICE

A sign that you have a happy marriage.

RING

If you are the recipient of a ring, someone is genuinely devoted to you. If you should break or lose a ring in your dream, someone with whom you have been intimate is losing interest in you.

ROCKET

A symbol of disappointment or that you sense the time has come to make some major changes in your life.

ROCKING CHAIR

Sitting in a rocking chair indicates feelings of instability.

ROOF

Being on a rooftop indicates your career has reached or soon will reach great heights.

ROSE

An unexpected joyous occasion. However, if the roses in your dreams

are withered, you may experience the loss of someone close to you. White roses generally are associated with illness—either your own or that of a loved one.

ROWBOAT

Riding in a rowboat signifies an active social life, but if the boat capsizes, expect a business failure that will lead to financial disaster.

RUNNING FOR ONE'S LIFE

A sign that you are afraid of someone or something. Another interpretation is that a woman who dreams of

being chased wishes to be pursued by a suitor.

S

SATAN
(See *Devil.*)

SAW

Operating a saw symbolizes that your home life is improving. But if the saw is rusty or broken, you may not be able to solve some family problems.

SCISSORS

A bad omen. Generally,

any dream involving scissors is associated with distrust in love affairs and marriages.

SCORPION

Danger. You have been involved in something scandalous that is close to erupting. If you are able to kill the scorpion in your dream, you will escape blame when the scandal is exposed.

SEX

Satisfying and pleasing sex indicates you are enjoying healthy relationships—whether with friends or a lover. If the sex in your dream is not fulfilling, there may be problems in a relationship. If you dream of watching others having sex, you need to form new relationships.

SHEEP

Associated with a successful career. The woollier the sheep, the more potential for success.

SICKNESS

Someone in your immediate family is in jeopardy. If you are sick in your dream, you may wish to examine your behavior—you may feel guilty about something you have been feeling, thinking, or doing.

SKELETON

Ill health—you may wish to consult a doctor or strive for a healthier lifestyle. If you are the skeleton in your dreams, you have been agonizing over something that is not really of great importance.

SLEEP

Sleeping in a clean and comfortable bed means

you are feeling at peace. If the bed is old, broken, or has dirty sheets, consider making some changes in your lifestyle.

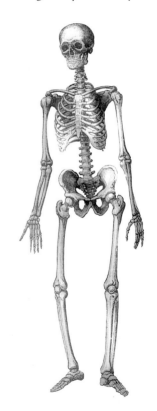

SLIDING OR SLIPPING

You will experience a major disappointment. This disappointment may manifest itself in a failed love affair or a business disaster.

SNAKES

If you are bitten by a snake, you will lose an important professional battle. If you kill the snake, you will succeed in a major struggle.

SNOW

You have been worrying unnecessarily about something.

SPACE

Dreams of outer space portend a break from a restrictive lifestyle to one that you find more liberating.

SPIDER

Careful and well-planned decisions are about to pay off.

SPLINTER

Splinters signify that you are envied by someone you consider a rival.

SQUIRREL

Who doesn't look forward to a visit from friends? Well, friends will soon be on their way to see you. If you happen to injure (accidentally or on purpose) a squirrel, you are in danger of losing a friend. If you dream of petting a squirrel, you and your family can expect years of joy.

STAIRS

Ascending a staircase signifies a path to personal and professional success. If you are descending or falling down the stairs, the path on which you are headed will take a sudden and unfortunate turn.

STALLION

Seeing a stallion or riding one portends a life of affluence and accomplishment.

STEALING

If you are stealing something, it's a sign that you should re-evaluate the way you have been treating others.

SUBWAY

Emotional distress.

SUN

If the sun is rising, you will soon accomplish great things. Seeing the sun at high noon means you are at a wonderful stage in your life. If the sun is setting, it is a sign you should guard your possessions carefully.

SWAMP

A rocky relationship will soon end.

SWIMMING

You are prepared for an important career change or a relocation.

T

TABLE

A table that is set with food and silverware means you will be reunited with a long-lost loved one. If the table is empty, you will

experience a period of loneliness and distress.

TAPEWORM
A warning that you will soon find yourself battling a health problem.

TEETH
Usually a sign of illness.

TELEPHONE
Hearing a telephone ring or speaking on a phone means you will soon meet a stranger who will have a major impact on your life.

TICKLE
Being tickled may indicate that you have an undiagnosed illness. If you are the tickler in the dream, you may be at risk of losing something valuable due to indiscretion or thoughtlessness.

TORNADO
A recent business decision was unwise.

TRAIN
You will soon need to make an unexpected trip. If the ride is quick and pleasant in your dream, your journey will be rewarding. If the train is crowded and the trip arduous, it would be wise to avoid any travel in the near future.

TRAMPOLINE
You have been on an emotional roller coaster lately. This ride is about to end. It is important to recall how you felt while you jumped on the trampoline. If you enjoyed the experience, you will find that your recent up-and-down feelings will end in a positive way. If, however, jumping on the

trampoline was an unpleasant experience, you may find yourself disappointed at the end of your struggles.

TUNNEL

Entering a tunnel means you will soon experience a major loss—either in your personal or professional life. Seeing a train in the tunnel indicates a period of grave illness.

TURKEY

There will be a major turn in your career. You can expect financial woes to cease and prosperity to ensue. If the turkeys are ill (or dead), your pride will be diminished by an upcoming business squabble. If the turkeys are in flight, you can expect your fiscal status to take a major turn for the better.

U

UMBRELLA

Carrying an umbrella in the rain signifies that you are experiencing a frustrating period in your life. If you are carrying an umbrella and it is not raining, it is a sign that you are accustomed to nuisances.

V

VALENTINE

Writing or sending valentines may mean you have recently developed feelings for a close friend that are stronger than you had realized.

VAMPIRE

Beware. Someone with whom you have recently become involved does not have your best interest in mind.

VASE

A vase filled with flowers portends a contented domestic life. If the vase is empty, your hopes for such a life will take more work than you had formerly realized.

VEIL

Wearing a veil may mean you have been unfaithful to your lover—either in thought or deed. If the veil is lifted, your infidelity will soon be discovered.

VINES

Expect a long period of prosperity.

VIOLIN

A good omen, indicating peace and love at home.

VOLCANO

Involvement in a harmful relationship that is characterized by jealousy and greed.

VULTURE

Beware of someone who may bring you harm. If you kill the vulture in your dream, you will escape the clutches of your enemy.

WALKING STICK

You have been, or will soon become, dependent upon others.

WASP

If you see a wasp or are stung by one, it is likely that someone is trying to manipulate you. If you kill the wasp, it is a sign you will manage to rid this person from your life.

WHEEL

The more quickly the wheel is spinning, the sooner you will achieve success. If the wheel is broken, you will find it difficult to achieve your goals.

WHISTLE

Hearing a whistle blow means that upsetting news will soon interrupt a pleasant period in your life. If, in your dream, you are blowing a whistle, you will make a sudden and significant change in your life.

WAGON

If the wagon is a covered one, your family will be plagued by many problems, and you will be the one most affected.

WINDOW

Open windows signify that you are responsive to your surroundings. You are feeling optimistic and open-minded about things that are new and foreign to you. If, however, the windows are closed or you are seeking to close them, you may be restricted by old habits that are not necessarily going to serve you well in the future.

WINGS

You are consumed with worry for a loved one who has recently moved.

WORM

You will soon be in a position where you must associate with people you do not like. If the worms are used as bait in your dream, you will be able to keep your professional distance from these people while maintaining your tact.

Y

YARDSTICK

Anxiety. Eliminate the things that are causing you the most stress and direct your energy towards what is truly important to you.